THE SECRET WORLD OF

Bears

THE SECRET WORLD OF

Bears

Rod Preston-Mafham

RAINTREE
Steck-Vaughn
PUBLISHERS

A Harcourt Company

Published by Raintree Steck-Vaughn Publishers, an imprint of Steck-Vaughn Company

Acknowledgments
Project Editors: Sean Dolan and Rebecca Hunter
Production Manager: Richard Johnson
Illustrated by Robert Morton
Designed by Ian Winton

Planned and produced by Discovery Books

Library of Congress Cataloging-in-Publication Data
Preston-Mafham, Rod
Bears / Rod Preston-Mafham
p. cm. -- (Secret world of--)
Includes bibliographical references (p.).
ISBN 0-7398-4983-2

Printed and bound in the United States
1 2 3 4 5 6 7 8 9 LB 05 04 03 02

Contents

CHAPTER 1
What Is a Bear?

A teddy bear may be a cuddly toy, but real bears are very dangerous animals. Bears are carnivorous, which means they belong to the group of mammals that feed mainly on meat, that is, on other animals. Other carnivores include cats, dogs, otters, and badgers. These mammals all look and behave quite differently, but the

Thick fur
For protection and warmth. Grows thicker for the winter

Bears are found in both North and South America, in Europe, and throughout much of Asia. They are not native to Africa, Australia, or Antarctica.

Of the approximately 240 species of carnivore in existence in the world today, only eight are bears.

The closest relations of the bear are the members of the dog, raccoon, and weasel families.

The polar bear is the largest land-based carnivore alive today.

▶ Bears are very heavily built animals with a large head. They have strong jaws, rather short legs, and big feet with long, sharp claws. Bears also have a large nose and a keen sense of smell, which helps them to find food and sense possible danger.

one thing that they nearly all have in common are two pairs of scissor-like back teeth, known as carnassials, that are used for slicing through the flesh of their prey.

THE BEAR FACTS

Today, there are eight species of bear alive. They range in size from the enormous polar bear, weighing around 1,320 pounds (600 kg), to the tiny sun bear that weighs only 143 pounds (65 kg). Despite these size differences, all bears have the same general appearance. All are heavily built animals with rather short legs and very short tails. Their heads are large, and in most species the snout is long. A bear's lips are not attached to its gums, so the lips are mobile and can be protruded. Bears have rather small ears and eyes so they cannot hear or see all that well, but they have a big nose and a great sense of smell.

Eyes
Sight is weak.

Nose
Very good sense of smell for finding food and identifying danger.

Sharp teeth
Large front teeth for tearing meat. Flat back teeth for chewing food.

Curved claws
Good for digging for food and climbing trees.

BEAR HABITATS

Most bears live in the cooler parts of the world, although the sun bear lives in the tropics. They tend to live in forested areas where the trees are not too dense. More open forest provides them with the variety of plants and animals on which they feed. The only one that does not live in forests is, of course, the polar bear, which lives on the Arctic ice sheets. One group of

Brown bears are found in the northern parts of North America, Europe, and Asia. This grizzly is at home in the snow-covered forests of Canada.

North American black bears can be found in the cypress forests of the Okefenokee Swamp on the borders of Georgia and Florida. Here they live quite happily, despite the fact that much of the area is flooded all year-round.

Like people, bears walk with their feet flat and their heels touching the ground. The soles of their feet are often hairy. Polar bears, in particular, need furry-soled feet to keep them from slipping on the smooth ice. Those species that climb trees, such as the black bear and the sloth bear, have hairless soles to their feet. Their foot pads have a rough surface that enables them to grip. Bears have broad, powerful paws with tough, thick claws for grasping food, digging, and defending their young.

Bears normally walk on all fours, but they can stand and walk on their hind legs—although rather clumsily. This ability to stand is useful because it helps them look out for danger or potential prey, which is important since their eyesight is poor. It also allows them to reach up to pick fruits and berries from trees.

Not a Bear!

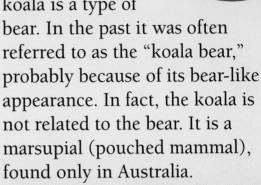

Many people mistakenly think that the koala is a type of bear. In the past it was often referred to as the "koala bear," probably because of its bear-like appearance. In fact, the koala is not related to the bear. It is a marsupial (pouched mammal), found only in Australia.

CHAPTER 2
The Origin of Bears

Around the time that dinosaurs became extinct, about 65 million years ago, carnivores first appeared and soon divided into the two families that we recognize today: the cats and their relations in one family, and the dogs, raccoons, weasels, and bears in the other.

True bears appeared on Earth about 20 million years ago.

Although bears are thought of as being carnivorous, most of them rely on a large percentage of plants in their diet.

The first bear-like animals lived on Earth about 34 million years ago. These creatures were about the size of a fox and lived in the forests of Asia, where they probably hunted in trees. After this early bear ancestor there is a big gap in the fossil record, until about 20 million years ago. By that time a creature clearly identifiable as a bear had evolved. This creature is regarded as the ancestor of all of today's modern bears. It is known as the Dawn Bear, and it was about 30 inches (75 cm) high at the shoulder. Like its ancestors, it probably spent a lot of its time in the trees.

EARLY BEARS
The first of these to appear were the pandas, about 20 million years ago. Fossils of several different species of early panda have been found. The oldest fossils of the present-day panda, however, are only 3 million years old. All known panda fossils have been discovered in China.

The ancestors of the spectacled bear are the next oldest species. They first appeared between 10 and 15 million years ago. These bears moved into more open areas, with fewer trees, and became fast-running hunters. Many species of this running bear evolved during the next few million years, especially in the Americas. Some of them, including the huge Florida cave bear, became vegetarian. Most of the running bears had died out by about 10,000 years ago, although the Florida cave bear may have hung on until about 8,000 years ago. The only living member of this group is the spectacled bear of South America, which has given up running and now lives mainly in the forests.

The earliest bears probably lived in the trees, and a few modern bears are still good climbers. Most bear species, such as this brown bear, are now too big to climb trees.

URSINE BEARS

The other six living species of bear are usually called the ursine bear. This name simply means "bear-like bears" and indicates that they are more typical bears. They started to appear 5 or 6 million years ago, when they were represented by the little bear. This was about the size of today's sun bear, but its scissor-like back teeth show that it was very much a meateater. Biologists believe that the little bear was the ancestor of the six types of living ursine bears and also of many extinct species known only from fossils.

A carving of a bear in stone that was crafted in Germany sometime between 15,000 and 10,000 B.C. Ancient people seem to have had a great respect for bears—carvings depicting them have been discovered in many different parts of the world where bears are found.

Some of these extinct bears were very large. They included the European cave bear, which was closely related to today's European brown bear but about three times as big. This large bear lived until about 10,000 years ago. It was well known to our own ancestors, who left paintings of the animals of their world on the walls of their caves.

These cave paintings show that bears were hunted by early humans. They would have used not only their meat, but their skins and bones too. In the cold Ice Age climate, bear skins would have made warm clothing and perhaps tent-like shelters. The bones of the bears could be made into weapons and tools such as needles.

Cave Bear Finds

The massive European cave bear was the most powerful Eurasian carnivore of its time. Its bones have been found in cave deposits all over Europe. Bears would hibernate in caves and often died during the winter. The bones were well-protected from the weather and scavengers, and so many sites have yielded huge quantities of bones. In one cave alone, 30,000 specimens were found. This skull of a cave bear was found in a cave in France.

I DIDN'T KNOW THAT

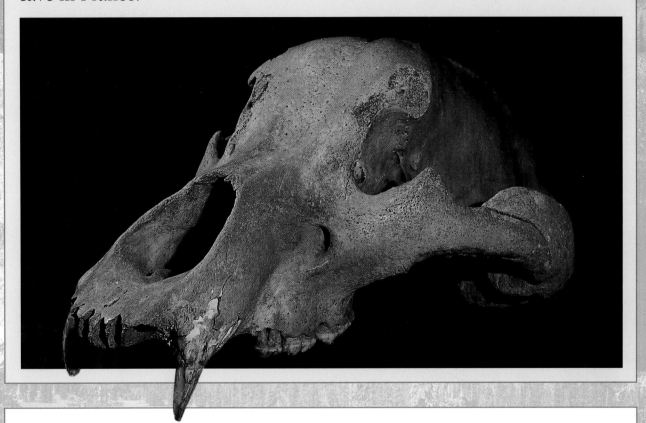

VEGETARIAN TEETH

Although the cave bears and some of the other descendants of the little bear became very large, they gradually turned from meat eating to a more omnivorous diet, rather like our own, with lots of vegetable matter. Along with this change of diet, their teeth began to change: the scissor-like carnassial teeth used for slicing through flesh gradually became less sharp and the surfaces of all the cheek teeth became flatter and more suitable for grinding up food from plants.

CHAPTER 3
Bears Today

Fully-grown male bears are always larger than females of the same species.

The largest of the purely land-dwelling bears is the Kodiak bear, a type of brown bear that can weigh up to 1,500 pounds (680kg).

When standing up, the tallest bear is the polar bear, which can reach 10 feet (3 m) in height. In contrast, the sun bear measures just under three feet (1 m) when upright.

The giant panda has an extra "thumb" on each hand. Often called the sixth claw, it is not a real thumb, but it can move like one. It helps the animal to grasp the bamboo stems on which it feeds. It is formed from one of the wrist bones and is covered with a callous pad.

GIANT PANDAS

With its thick, woolly, black and white fur, and black eyes and ears, the giant panda cannot be mistaken for any other bear. It is one of the smallest bears, with a maximum male weight of about 275 pounds (125 kg) and height of about 4 feet (1.2 m). When it was first discovered by scientists, it was considered to be related either to the racoon or the much

With its black and white fur, the panda bear is instantly recognizable. In Wolong Reserve in southwest China, a panda bear digs into a meal of bamboo, its main source of food in the wild.

smaller red panda. More recently, chemical analysis of the giant panda's tissues shows that it is much more closely related to the bear family. The giant panda was once found in many places in China, but widespread destruction of its habitat—bamboo forests—has left it confined to only a few remote forests in southwest China.

SPECTACLED BEARS

It is easy to see how this bear got its name. A spectacled bear is usually dark brown in color, with lighter fur around the eyes that give it the appearance of wearing spectacles!

Spectacled bears are so called because of the white markings found around the eyes. These markings can vary greatly on individual bears.

The spectacled bear is the only species native to South America, where it is found in the mountains of Venezuela, Colombia, Peru, and Ecuador. It lives mainly in forests, but sometimes in the montane grassland above the tree level.

Male spectacled bears can get quite large, weighing up to 340 pounds (155 kg) and standing up to 5 feet (1.5 m) tall.

POLAR BEARS

The largest and most easily recognized of the ursine bears is the polar bear, which lives in the Arctic region of the northern hemisphere. The polar bear is the youngest bear, evolving into its present form about 2 million years ago. It is believed to have evolved from a population of large brown bears that had not completely given up their original carnivorous habits. The fact that polar bears and brown bears can interbreed shows that they are very closely related. The huge polar bear is covered with dense, water-repelling white fur on top of a black skin. It has an excellent sense of smell and can bound across the ice at great speed. It is semi-aquatic and spends much of its life hunting for food in the icy waters of the Arctic Ocean. Polar bears have been found swimming many miles from the nearest land. A 4-inch (10-cm)-thick layer of fat, or blubber, under the skin ensures that the bear keeps warm even in the coldest conditions.

Because of poor eyesight, bears rely heavily on their sense of smell to find food. This polar bear, in Arctic Norway, stands on its hind legs and sniffs the air, perhaps trying to pick up the scent of a seal.

Brown Bears

The brown bear, also known as the grizzly bear in America, lives in the Rockies and the Pacific Northwest of North America, in parts of Europe, and throughout much of the northern part of Asia. Although they are called brown bears, they can in fact be almost any color between black and pale cream. In the Pamir and Tien Shan Mountains of Central Asia, some of the cream-colored bears also have pale claws instead of dark brown ones. These pale bears have been given the name of Isabelline, or white-clawed, bears. It was once thought that there were many species or kinds of brown bear, but we now know that they all belong to a single, very variable species.

Kodiak Bears

The largest brown bears are the Kodiak bears that live on the Kodiak islands of Alaska. The males can weigh as much as 1,500 pounds (680 kg). At the other end of the scale, the brown bears living in the Spanish Pyrenees weigh only about 650 pounds (280 kg).

The grizzly bear, the American form of the brown bear, is usually a loner. These three, however, are in the McNeil River Bear Sanctuary in Alaska, where they have undoubtably come together to feed upon the salmon swimming upstream to spawn.

BLACK BEARS

The American black bear is found over much of the United States and Canada. This bear is usually black, with a paler muzzle, but it can also be brown, reddish-brown, or bluish-black. So how do you tell a brown bear from a black bear? In general, black bears are smaller than brown bears. Brown bears also have a hump at the shoulders and are more aggressive than black bears. Black bears are skillful tree climbers, but brown bears, being heavier, are not.

The Asian black bear can be found in various places on the continent of Asia, including northern India and Nepal, parts of Kampuchea (Cambodia), China, Laos, Thailand, Vietnam, and some Japanese islands. It is also found in the very far east of Russia, in the forest of the

Despite their large size, American black bears are good climbers. They climb trees to find food and to escape from danger. The long, sharp claws typical of bears are clearly visible on the front paws of this bear.

18

High-Speed Bears

Bears may look slow and clumsy, but they can actually run very fast. The American black bear can run at speeds of up to 25 miles (40 km) per hour when chasing prey. Even faster are polar bears, which can reach up to 35 miles (56 km) per hour. This is fast enough to allow them to run down a reindeer, and they can easily outrun a person. They can also swim at up to 6 miles (10 km) per hour. However, bears cannot run at these high speeds for more than a few minutes. Their thick fur and blubber make them too hot.

region called Ussuriland, which borders China and Korea. It is roughly the same size as the American black bear but has noticeably bigger ears and a band of pale fur across its chest. Although called a black bear, in some areas its shaggy coat is more brown in color. The Asian black bear is also an excellent tree climber. Studies of these bears in the wild have found that they live for a considerable length of time, 24 years being the average lifespan.

SLOTH BEARS

The sloth bear and the sun bear are both small bears and are both nocturnal. The sloth bear is found primarily in Sri Lanka and India. Its long, shaggy black hair and pale muzzle and chest patch make it instantly recognizable. Although small in relation to other bears, males can still weigh as much as 310 pounds (140 kg) and stand up to 5 feet (1.5 m) tall. The sloth bear is an expert climber and, with the aid of its big claws, can hang upside-down from the branches like a sloth! Although normally nocturnal, there is some evidence to show that mother sloth bears with cubs come out during the day. If this is so, it may be because they are trying to stay out of the way of tigers and leopards, which come out at night to hunt.

SUN BEARS

The smallest of all bears, the sun bear, is also black. It has very small ears and short fur—suited to its life in the tropics. It has a gray muzzle and a pale-colored patch on its chest, which varies a lot from bear to

Despite its long, shaggy hair, the sloth bear is usually found in the tropics. The sloth bear lives mainly on insects, but it also enjoys fruit, eggs, and honey. This one lives in India.

bear. This patch often spreads across the chest in a distinct U-shape, but in some bears it is almost nonexistent. This bear lives in the forests of Malaysia, Burma, Thailand, Cambodia, Vietnam, Laos, Borneo, and Sumatra.

The sun bear is the world's smallest bear, measuring about 4 feet (1.2 m) from head to tail. It is easily recognizable by the U-shaped mark across its chest.

CHAPTER 4
Food and Feeding

The polar bear is the only bear species that is primarily a meat eater. It is, therefore, the only bear with well-developed slicing, carnassial teeth.

The spectacled bear is particularly fond of fruit and is a good climber. It plays an important role in the forest by spreading the seeds of the trees from which it feeds.

Sloth bears dig holes in termite mounds, blow away the loose dust, and then suck the termites into their mouth, like a vacuum cleaner.

The polar bear has a huge stomach. It can eat as much as one fifth of its body weight at a single meal.

Although bears are carnivores, they are known to eat almost anything. Since many are omnivorous, they will eat a mixture of meat and plants. Their teeth show how they have evolved, or adapted, to handle this mixed diet. All bears have pointed canine teeth, like those of a cat or dog, that are used to grip and hold onto their prey. They also have broad, flat molars, somewhat like our own, that are suited for chewing up food from plants.

Bears are always on the lookout for something to eat. This black bear has used its powerful claws to tear its way into a bees' nest so it can feed on the grubs and honey inside. Its thick fur will protect it from the stings of the angry bees.

OMNIVOROUS DIETS

The brown bear, the black bear, the sun bear, and the spectacled bear will eat almost anything edible that they encounter. Leaves, fruits, and berries make up about 80 percent of the brown bear's diet. The rest consists of live or dead animals including insects, worms, fish, rodents, and occasional larger mammals, such as deer.

Bears have to be able to take advantage of seasonal foods, such as young shoots and leaves in spring and fruits and berries in the fall. This grizzly bear is feasting on a patch of blueberries in the Denali National Park, Alaska.

Brown bears are very adaptable in their diet. If meat, including fish, is available, brown bears will readily eat it, but in areas where meat is scarce they rely more on plants.

FRUIT AND NUTS

Black bears feed much like the brown bears. What they eat varies with their location and with the season. Springtime provides them with buds and fresh young leaves, while the fall brings an abundance of all kinds of fruit with which they can fatten themselves up before winter.

The spectacled bear feeds largely on fruit and has jaws strong

An American black bear in the Rocky Mountains enjoys the berries on an ash tree in winter. Being able to stand on two legs is a great advantage when reaching for fruit.

enough to break open tough nuts. Like the other bears, however, spectacled bears will eat any animals that they can catch or kill, and they do not object to eating carrion (dead animals).

Less is known about the diet of the sun bear. It uses its long tongue to extract all kinds of insects, especially termites, from their hiding places. The sun bear can be a nuisance on plantations, where it feeds on the young buds of bananas and coconut palms.

Like the sloth bear, the sun bear is a very good climber and there is some evidence that it even sleeps up in the trees. Sadly, sun bear cubs are sometimes taken as pets by local people. At 4 or 5 years of age, however, they can no longer be trusted as pets and so are either killed or released back into the wild. Not knowing how to get food, it is doubtful that they survive for long.

Like most bears, the sun bear feeds on a mixture of plants and animals. Its very long tongue helps it to extract termites and other insects and their grubs from the nooks and crannies in which they hide.

HUNTING AND FISHING

The two largest types of bear, the brown bear and the polar bear, have a diet that is rich in meat. The grizzly bears of North America and Siberia seem to enjoy fishing for salmon when the fish are swimming up the rivers to spawn. The bears get together, often in large numbers, in areas where the rivers are fairly shallow and the fish are easy to catch. Here, they gorge themselves on the very nutritious salmon. Old-timers pick the best spots for fishing and will drive off any other bear that tries to muscle in. Young bears are easily picked out as they flounder about, trying desperately to grab hold of the slippery fish. By watching the older bears, the young bears soon learn how and where to fish.

A brown bear reaches out, jaws wide open, to catch a salmon as it jumps up a waterfall on its way upstream to its spawning site. During this season, fish are a very important part of the bear's diet.

Polar Bear Diet

The polar bear eats hardly anything but meat. During the winter months it catches ringed seals, by waiting next to the holes in the ice where the seals come up to breathe. When the seal appears, the bear grabs it with a huge paw and throws it up on to the ice. The bears will also actively hunt, often traveling as much as 50 miles (80 km) a day across ice floes in search of seals.

Summer Hunting

Most animals eat well in the summer months in order to fatten up for the winter, when less food is available. The polar bear does the opposite. In the Arctic, there is

Polar bears are the most carnivorous of the bears. This young bear has caught a ringed seal, its main prey, and is in the process of eating it. First it will eat the outer layers of skin and fatty blubber and then, if it is really hungry, it will eat the red meat.

plenty of food available in the winter, but polar bears have a difficult time hunting in the summer when the sea ice melts. In the summer, they rely on stored body fat and scavenge on anything else that comes their way. Fruit may be part of their diet at this time, as are seabirds and their eggs and young. In summer, some towns in Alaska and northern Canada have problems with polar bears that come into town to raid garbage dumps. This creates a big safety problem for the people who live there.

DIETS

the giant panda has the carnivorous habits of tors, its digestive system is still not very efficient at dealing with plant material. The animal has to eat a lot of bamboo— perhaps 20 pounds (9 kg) each day—in order to get enough nourishment from it. Apart from an occasional rodent and a few insects, it does not appear to eat meat, but this could be because there are very few animals the slow-moving panda could catch. even if it wanted to.

ANT EATER

Another special feeder is the sloth bear, with a diet consisting mainly of ants and termites. It has long claws and powerful front teeth for breaking logs and getting to insects and other invertebrates. Its long sticky tongue mops up its insect food easily. Alternatively, having made a hole in a termite mound, the sloth bear blows out any dust and then sucks up the termites like a vacuum cleaner. While they are sucking up the termites, the sloth bears make an

A sloth bear using its enormous strength and long claws to tear open a termite mound to get at the grubs and workers inside. This is not as easy to do as you may think … termites cement their nest mound together as it is built and it is as hard as rock.

Placid Pandas

If pandas were any more active, they would run out of energy and die. This is because they obtain very little energy from their food. Pandas, therefore, are not very active animals and spend a lot of time sitting around, doing nothing in particular. Most of their life is spent moving from one patch of food to another, eating, resting, and then moving on to the next source of food.

extraordinary noise. It is said that this noise is so loud it can be heard from a distance of 330 feet (100 m) or more. Getting at their termite food and sucking it up stir up a lot of dust. The bears are able to close their nostrils to prevent the dust from getting up their

noses. Termite-feeding animals are not very common throughout the sloth bear's range, so good supplies of the insect are usually available all year. The sloth bear will also eat fruit when it is in season, as well as flowers, grass, eggs, and honey.

CHAPTER 5
Reproduction

Bears begin breeding between 3 and 6 years of age depending on the species.

Although they can start breeding at a younger age, male polar bears and Alaskan brown bears do not reach their maximum size until they are about 11 years old.

Newborn bears are very small, compared to their mothers. The mother panda is 800 times as heavy as her newborn cubs. In comparison, human mothers are about 15 times as heavy as their babies at birth.

Bears produce a milk that is very rich in fat, so their cubs grow fast once they are born. Polar bear milk contains as much as 40 percent fat, compared with about 4–5 percent for cow's milk.

GETTING TOGETHER

Bears like to live alone. They seek out each other's company only when males and females are ready to mate. A female bear will leave scent marks as she moves about looking for food. These let wandering male bears know that she is around. Once a male bear has found a female, he may visit her over a period of several days until she is finally ready to mate with him. Polar bear couples will stay together for a few days and mate more than once. Where groups of polar bears gather at mating time, as happens in some areas, males may mate with more than one female and females with more than one male.

Though bears live alone for most of their adult life, males and females have to get together in order to produce young. Here, a male Alaskan brown bear approaches a female in hopes that she will allow him to mate with her.

GIVING BIRTH

The gestation period—the time during which the babies develop inside their mothers—ranges from 16 to 39 weeks. Big bears take longer to develop than small bears. Most bears produce one or two cubs, but occasionally up to four may be born. The mother gives birth in the safety of a den. Polar bear cubs are born in the middle of winter, in a den dug deep in a

Like most mammals, female bears are very good mothers and spend a great deal of time taking care of and looking after their young. Here, a Eurasian brown bear cub is licking its mother's nose, perhaps letting her know it's hungry.

snowdrift. The newborn cubs are blind, helpless, and usually lacking any fur. Panda, polar bear, and spectacled bear cubs, however, do have a thin layer of fur when they are born.

Bear Cubs

The cubs stay with their mother in the den for the first few weeks of their lives. During this time, the female does not go out to feed but busies herself with grooming, cleaning, and feeding her cubs. The young cubs do not have very much hair at first and so she must stay with them to keep them warm, like a bird sitting on its chicks in the nest. She keeps the den clean and tidy until they are all ready to leave. By then, the mother may

A mother polar bear and her two cubs outside the den in which they were born. Perhaps this is the cubs' first sight of the world of ice and snow in which they will spend the rest of their lives.

have lost one-third of her weight because she has not been out to feed, having remained with her cubs.

Eventually, mother and cubs leave the den so that she can hunt for food. The cubs follow their mother around, learning from her what is edible and how to catch their own food. One thing that the mother bear has to do, which may seem rather odd, is to keep her cubs away from male bears. It is quite common for a male bear to kill young cubs. Female bears will actively defend their cubs against the male, even though he is usually much bigger than she. Many cubs are quite good at climbing trees, and their mother will often send them up a tree to keep them safe while she chases off the male.

Once they are large enough to look after themselves, the cubs are abandoned by their mother as she goes off on her own, leaving them to make their own way in the world.

Follow the Leader

Once they leave the den in which they were born, it is normal for bear cubs to follow their mother around until they can look after themselves. Most bear cubs walk beside their mother, but a sloth bear mother allows her cubs to ride around on her back.

CHAPTER 6
Bear Behavior

Bears are big and need a lot to eat. This is one of the reasons why they are solitary animals. If too many bears lived in a particular area, food would soon become scarce, leading to fighting and probably the eventual death of the weaker bears. Most bears have no real enemies, apart from people. This means they can largely look after themselves and do not need the protection offered by a group.

Male bears will often stand on their hind legs to make themselves look bigger, when they are competing with other males for a female.

Like most mammals, young bears spend much time playing with one another. This teaches them some of the behavior patterns that they will need when they are grown up.

Lone bears have been seen "playing" on their own. In particular, both American black bears and pandas sometimes slide down snowy slopes, as if they were sledding!

A male Kodiak brown bear threatening another male, out of view of the camera. This aggressive behavior is normally only seen during the breeding season, when two or more males are vying for a single female.

Bear Talk

Unlike their close relatives in the dog family, bears are relatively quiet creatures. However, they do produce a number of sounds, which seem to have particular meanings. In general, it seems that the greatest amount of "talking" takes place with forest-dwelling bears, where keeping track of one another among the trees is more difficult. Polar bears, with their habitat on the open ice, rarely use this form of communication with one another.

One of the most common sounds, the roar, is produced by all bears. It means that the animal is feeling angry, and it serves as a warning to others to stay out of its way. Mother bears produce sounds to keep in contact with their cubs.

Play is important in helping young mammals learn some of the skills that they will need later in adult life. These two young brown bears appear to be engaged in a tussle over a tree branch.

The cubs, in turn, make sounds that the mother understands. Both spectacled and sloth bear cubs have been heard to squeal or yelp, when they are in trouble.

Playing

Like most baby mammals, bear cubs play with each other a great deal. During this play, they are practicing the kinds of things they will have to do when they leave their mother: searching for food, killing prey, running from danger, and how to behave when they meet other bears. Play-fighting is very prevalent, even in nearly fully-grown cubs, but it is stopped before the bears hurt one another.

Winter Sleep

Whether a bear sleeps through much of the winter depends upon its food supply. Pandas and spectacled, sloth, and sun bears, which all live in warm climates, have food available throughout the year and do not sleep through winter. Polar bears thrive during the winter when their main food —seals—is abundant. They do, however, slow down a bit in summertime.

It is the two species of black bear and brown bear that sleep for part of the winter. The further north a bear lives, the longer it sleeps. Brown bears living in the far north of North America, for example, can sleep for as long as seven months of the year, while

Spring has arrived, the snow is beginning to melt, and this brown bear is now emerging from its winter den.

American black bears in the south of their range may sleep for as little as two weeks. The bears fatten themselves up during the fall so that they have enough stored food in their bodies to tide them through the winter. Brown bears often dig their own dens in the side of a hill, though they will also use piles of brushwood or logs. American black bears prefer hollow trees, but they too will use piles of brushwood or even small caves.

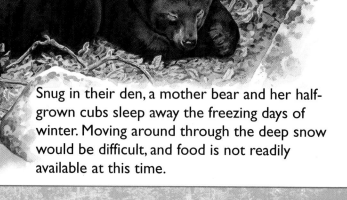

Snug in their den, a mother bear and her half-grown cubs sleep away the freezing days of winter. Moving around through the deep snow would be difficult, and food is not readily available at this time.

The bears' winter sleep is sometimes called hibernation, but it is not nearly such a deep sleep as that of other animals, such as the woodchuck and some ground squirrels. The body temperature of these animals drops to within a few degrees of freezing, and other bodily activities slow almost to a stop. This is true hibernation and the animals take a long time to awaken from it. The temperature of sleeping bears, however, drops by only a few degrees and the animals take only a few minutes to wake up.

Keeping Cool

The thick layer of insulating fat that keeps polar bears warm in the icy Arctic waters is a problem for them in summer. It makes it very difficult for them to keep cool. One way they solve this is by lying down on the remaining patches of ice or by spending more time in the water.

I DIDN'T KNOW THAT

CHAPTER 7

Bears and People

The panda, the most identifiable bear of all, has been adopted as the emblem of the World Wildlife Fund (WWF), an organization that works to protect wildlife around the world. Although the panda has become a symbol of conservation, it is considered to be endangered, as are five other bear species. Only the polar bear and American black bear are considered currently safe from the threat of extinction.

The earliest known examples of cave drawings of bears are estimated to be about 35,000 years old.

Six states in the United States have a bear as their emblem. The grizzly is the official state animal of California.

About 6,000 European brown bears live in the mountain forests of Transylvania, where they are fully protected by Romanian law.

In the past, bears have not been treated very kindly by humans, and things are not much better today. In Poland, Romania, and Russia, bears are still taught to dance and perform other tricks.

An organization called "Libearty" was formed in 1992. Its goal is to protect bears around the world from cruel treatment by humans.

This captive sloth bear is used by its handler in India to entertain tourists. Sloth bears are an endangered species.

Humans and bears have interacted for thousands of years. The fellow-feeling we have for these animals may arise from the fact that, like us, they often stand up and walk on their hind legs. From a distance, they can even resemble a human being. In the past, humans in certain cultures, especially Native Americans, may have worshiped bears.

The Inuit people, in the far north of America, have had a long history of living with the polar bear.

Taking great care, for polar bears are dangerous animals, the Inuit still hunt bears for both meat and skins—the latter being the best material for making warm, snow-proof pants. The Inuit continue to admire and respect these animals, and many still consider polar bear hunting to be a test of manhood.

The native peoples of the Arctic regions have traditionally hunted polar bears for their skins and meat and are still allowed to do so under controlled conditions. Here, polar bear skins are hung out to dry in northwestern Greenland.

A cuddly teddy bear is often a child's first toy. This friendly and lovable image of bears is reinforced by characters from children's books and television, such as Winnie the Pooh, Paddington, and Yogi Bear. In real life, however, bears are not friendly toward humans and can be very dangerous. Most dangerous of all is a mother bear with cubs that she feels are being threatened.

PROBLEM BEARS

As the worldwide human population increases, our contact with bears also increases. Bears' habitats are invaded and often destroyed by people, as human settlement expands. In North America, for example, bears are becoming something of a nuisance in many areas. Constant contact with humans reduces their fear, and they come into towns and homes to forage for food. In national parks in the United States, bear-proof garbage cans are provided.

In northern Canada, a mother polar bear plods along, with her two half-grown cubs following behind. They seem to be unaware that they are being watched by interested tourists in the vehicles in the background.

These Asian black bear cubs are behind bars, but not for doing anything wrong. Had they not been rescued from their captors in Thailand, their flesh would have been eaten and other parts of their bodies used in traditional medicine.

Campers are encouraged not to leave food in tents but to hang it high in a tree, to keep it out of range.

The other side of the coin is that this increased tolerance of humans means more people get a chance to see bears in the wild. Thousands of tourists visit Churchill in northern Canada to see the polar bears that congregate there each year, and special bear-proof vehicles have been built so that the tourists can get within just a few feet of the bears.

In Alaska, watching brown bears as they catch salmon from the rivers has become so popular that restrictions have been placed on the number of people that can watch them at any one time.

ILLEGAL MEDICINES

In parts of Asia, bears are killed to obtain parts of their bodies for use in medicines. The most important part is the animal's gall bladder. Often a bear is killed, the gall bladder removed, and the rest of the animal left to rot. In some Asian countries, bears are specially bred for their bile, which is the substance produced by the gall bladder in the liver. These captive-bred bears live in cramped, unhealthy conditions.

CHAPTER 8
Conservation

Five of the eight species of bear are in danger of becoming extinct in the relatively near future, unless steps are taken to protect and conserve them.

Only four species of bear are actively protected in the wild. Of these, the American black, the brown, and the polar bear are reasonably safe, but the panda is still in great danger of becoming extinct.

Some efforts are being made to protect the spectacled bear in northeast South America, but lack of funding is not helping the project in poorer countries.

Because not much is known about it, there has been little interest in conserving the sun bear, though some research on this species is now being undertaken in Borneo.

So how many bears are left in the world today? The American black bear is the most numerous, with a population of between 400,000 and 500,000, followed by the brown bear, with about 50,000 in North America and 70,000 in Europe and Asia combined. Polar bears are not easy to count, because of their remote habitat. Estimates of their numbers can vary from 5,000 to 12,000. There are fewer than 10,000 sloth bears left in the wild, and an unknown number of sun bears, so both species are considered to be endangered. This is also true of the Asiatic black bear, for which there are no figures available. At the bottom of the list is the spectacled bear, which numbers less than 2,000 in the wild, and the

People are beginning to realize that unless something is done about it, there will soon be no bears left in the wild. The grizzly bear now safely resides in the vast national parks that have been set up in the United States and Canada.

The Teddy Bear

The term "teddy bear" originates with U.S. President Theodore "Teddy" Roosevelt. An enthusiastic outdoorsman, President Roosevelt was invited on a bear hunt in the Mississippi Delta in November 1902. His hosts captured a bear and tied it to a tree, then encouraged Roosevelt to shoot it. The president thought this was unsportsmanlike and refused to shoot the bear. The incident was soon the subject of a cartoon in the *Washington Post* and drew nationwide attention. Enterprising businesspeople began manufacturing stuffed bears; the popular new toys were called "teddy bears" in honor of the president.

panda, with only 1,100 in the wild. Unless steps are taken to preserve bear habitats and protect bears from poaching, the world may lose some of these valuable and extraordinary creatures forever.

Much attention has been brought to the work being done in China and in zoos around the world to protect the panda. What is being done for other bears? In 1965, representatives of the countries where polar bears live met and came to an agreement on how the polar bear should be protected. Most other species of bear receive some form of protection, even if this is only in limited areas within national parks or nature reserves. The only answer to the problem of bear conservation is to teach people about these creatures and how valuable they are to our world. Since many bears now live in areas that people want to claim for their own living space, this will not be an easy feat!

Glossary

CANINES – Long pointed teeth at the front of the mouth

CARNASSIAL – Describes carnivore cheek teeth, which have a sharp, cutting ridge for slicing up meat

CARNIVORE – An animal that eats meat

DEN – A cozy hiding place, such as a cave, where mother bears give birth to their cubs and some species of bear spend the cold winter months

DIGITS – Fingers and toes

ENDANGERED – Likely to become extinct in the wild in the near future

EVOLVE – To change gradually over a long period of time

EXTINCT – When a species of animal no longer exists today

FOSSILS – The remains or trace of a living thing that has been preserved in rock

HERBIVORE – An animal that eats plants

INCISOR TEETH – The teeth at the very front of the jaw

MAMMALS – Animals with fur, whose young feed on milk produced by the mother

MUZZLE – The protruding front of the face of a bear that contains the teeth and nose

NOCTURNAL – Describing animals that are active at night

OMNIVORE – An animal that eats both animals and plants

PREDATOR – An animal that catches and eats other animals

PREY – An animal that is caught and eaten by another animal

SOLITARY – Living alone

SPECIES – Scientific name given to describe a particular kind of animal

URSINE – Describes the group to which most bears belong, except for the panda and spectacled bear

Further Reading

Feeney, Kathy. *Black Bears*. Minnetonka, MN: Creative Publishing International, 2000.

Lynch, Wayne. *Bears, Bears, Bears*. Buffalo, NY: Firefly Books, 1995.

Patent, Dorothy Hinshaw. *The Way of the Grizzly*. St. Louis, MO: Clarion, 1991.

Robinson, Claire. *Bears*. Chicago: Heinemann Library, 1998.

Acknowledgments

Cover: Daniel J Cox/Oxford Scientific Films; p. 8: Andy Rouse/Natural History Photographic Agency; p. 9: John Shaw/Bruce Coleman Collection; p. 11: Konrad Wothe/Oxford Scientific Films; p. 12: Ancient Art & Architecture; p.13: Daniel Heuclin/Musee Lecoq/Natural History Photographic Agency; p.s 14 & 15: Jorg & Petra Wegner/Bruce Coleman Collection; p. 16: Andy Rouse/Natural History Photographic Agency; p. 17: Johnny Johnson/Bruce Coleman Collection; p. 18: Rich Kirchner/Natural History Photographic Agency; p. 19: Dan Gurarich/Oxford Scientific Films; p. 20: Rod Williams/ Bruce Coleman Collection; p. 21: Mike Hill/Oxford Scientific Films; p.s 22/23 & 24: T Kitchin & V Hurst/ Natural History Photographic Agency; p. 25: Jorg & Petra Wegner/Bruce Coleman Collection; p. 26: Hans Reinhard/Bruce Coleman Collection; p. 27: Dan Gurarich/Oxford Scientific Films; p. 29: James Warwick/Natural History Photographic Agency; p.: 30 Daniel J Cox/Oxford Scientific Films; p. 31: Gerard Lacz/Natural History Photographic Agency; p. 32: Andy Rouse/Natural History Photographic Agency; p. 33: David E Myers/Natural History Photographic Agency; p. 34: Hans Reinhard/Bruce Coleman Collection; p. 35: Dr. Eckart Pott/Bruce Coleman Collection; p. 37: Konrad Wothe/Oxford Scientific Films; p. 37: Dr. Eckart Pott/Bruce Coleman Collection; p. 38: Kevin Schafer/Natural History Photographic Agency; p. 39: B & C Alexander/Natural History Photographic Agency; p. 40: Kevin Schafer/Natural History Photographic Agency; p. 41: Andy Rouse/Natural History Photographic Agency; p. 42: David Middleton/Natural History Photographic Agency. All background images © Steck-Vaughn Collection (Corbis Royalty Free, Getty Royalty Free, and StockBYTE).

Index

Numbers in *italic* indicate pictures